Uncharted Waters

Mallory Williams

BookLeaf
Publishing

India | USA | UK

Presentation by *BookLeaf Publishing*

Web: www.bookleafpub.com

E-mail: info@bookleafpub.com

ISBN: 9789357449090

First edition 2022

DEDICATION

To:

The little girl who grew up too fast

The girl who hid behind a book for too long

The tween who never thought she would be
loved

The teenager who struggled to find her way out
of the dark

The young adult who feared being alone with
her thoughts

And

The adult who is finally figuring out who she is

This collection is for them because I want them
to know just how much we have grown.

ACKNOWLEDGEMENT

To those who wiped away my tears,
To those who carried me when I couldn't bear to
stand,
To those who lit the way in the dark,
To those who lent an ear,
To those who held my hand,
To those who housed my heart.

Even if our paths crossed for only a moment,
I cannot thank you enough.

PREFACE

Articulating feeling has never been a strength of mine.
I spent too long holding back the words.

Now, I struggle to explain feelings to myself, let alone others.
I've always waited for the words to come on their own.
Never testing, never pushing, all in the name of comfort.

But no more.
I will find the words, and I will force them into being.
It's a lot easier to make sense of a puzzle you can see.

I will take all these pieces and put together a picture of who I was, who I am, and who I want to be.

Someone Smash Some Champagne

I am lost without a map to who I want to be.
All I know is I've been here before-
The scenery has changed as time passed us by,
But then again, I guess I've changed too.

I walk along the edge of all I have ever known.
It is peaceful and kind and I hate to leave it
behind,
But there is nothing left for me to do that would
do me any good.
It is too early to stop, too late to stay, and
standing still is a waste of time.

And so I am off, sailing in this boat of hope that
I have made,
wondering if it will be enough to brave the
uncharted waters.

A Stargazer's Sonnet

A story's birth fell on the clearest night
Connecting dots to make an image new
The sky is vast and full of shining light
I hope my nearing future's brighter too.

The constellations cannot be my guide.
Without them I am surely sailing blind,
The risks I take, they cannot be denied
The path is mine to make and mine to find.

I wrestle with the cooling of the air
And wondering how long these journeys last.
Will I survive without somebody there
To hold me close until the storm has passed?

Determination's glint rose in my eyes
For I am strong, yes, I am of the skies.

Sea Shanties

How does one pass the time?
On the days where seconds contain eternities
with no land in sight,
I wanted to forget everything and drift without
direction.
Even forgetting couldn't change time itself.

Melodies ring in my ears, softer than a lullaby,
memories flash but the words never come.
Can I articulate my pain into song as though it
were stained glass,
and not a shattered mirror?

Sweeter Sorrow

The hardest splash will create the largest ripples,
but even ripples die.
Dive too deep into isolation and you will find
that the loudest cry will never be heard.

The softest tear fell and all I wanted was to be
seen,
to see someone I know and be able to feel their
care without pretense.
Try too hard to read into something and you will
find
that the kindest gesture can never be genuine-
even when it is.

These are the sweeter sorrows,
for isn't it better to feel sadness than nothing at
all?

Stalagmites

I have known some stalagmites in my time,
wherein when I say stalagmite, I am referring to
rock bottom.

Have you ever been at rock bottom?
It's dark and cold and lonely,
But there's nowhere to go but up I suppose.

Some suggest this change in perspective when
you find yourself below,
from which I arrive to two conclusions:

They have never felt the crushing weight of the
sea above
or
They have found themselves in a position to
forget.

I do not envy either, for I have emerged from the
depth without hope of aid.
Indeed, I have learned to trust that I am a strong
swimmer.

Setting Sun

Goodbyes have never been my forte,
I'd hold the sun hostage overhead if I was able.

I would spend the night in a lover's mourning,
clothed in darkness thick enough to block out
the advances of the moon.
He is a beauty I never allowed myself to
appreciate until he was gone.

But now, I bask in the light,
sun and moon alike.

I've gotten better at letting go since then,
though here and now, I've no reason to worry-
I know that he's always coming back.

But still I cannot bring myself to proceed
without reservation,
I have yet to get through my first new moon.

Swaying

I get nauseous on boats.
I get nauseous at home in my bed.
I get seasick with sea legs that I can't keep still.

I do not know when it will come, but I do know
that it is coming.
It comes back in like the tide without
somewhere to be.

Stumbling

When too much comes knocking in your
window,
you are blown away and struggle to stand.

It holds you down to prove that you are not
enough,
at least until apathy pulls you through the floor.

As you walk away, you stumble ever so slightly,
for your strength and faith in solid ground have
been taken from you.

Settling

The anchor is away, for now.
To move on it is important to remember that
sometimes we must remain stagnant.
Growth without rest is a guaranteed dejection.

There comes a time at which we must all drop
anchor;
A day when we cannot keep ourselves upright
long enough to stay the course,
A day when downwind is whence we came.

Stowaways

I found my hope tied to the mast.
I found my sorrow weighing me down.

My anxiety was busy rocking the boat.
My fear was about to drop the anchor.

Trust and faith were clinging to the ship's side.
Uncertainty was up in the air, shifting sails on a
whim.

Amidst the chaos of protecting everything else,
I failed to catch myself and fell overboard.

Sink or Swim

In suspension we lay,
Waiting for the opportunity to fly away.
Can we bear to stay,
And live to see another day?

Another wave crashes overhead,
We're losing the strength to tread.
With solace to find in the fishes' bed,
Should we try to change instead?

It's time to choose with no way back,
to glow above or fade to black.

Safety

I break the surface and claw for a breath of air
alone.
Invigoration's gift lifts me back to where I
started,
and for a moment I am discouraged.
Only a moment.

I shiver and the sun leaves the sky to wrap me in
warmth.
With security comes the notion that I am no
longer alone-
I never was.

Call it naivete, call it denial.
I thought I could move on, forgetting all that
shackled me ashore.
You cannot grow and leave yourself behind.

Starlight's Solace

For the first time, it is only the night that is
broken-
I have found my missing pieces and held them
together
with the best bowline knot I can muster.

Siren's Song

I woke to the call of my homeland,
to return once more to the simple monotony.

The urge grew as I was smaller and smaller,
wrapped in the shame of wanting defeat.

One more day,
I can give myself one more day.

Seven

All these seas surround,
Filled with fear and fortitude.
Can you see the waves?

Shoreline

There ahead lies what I have been dreaming of,
the promise of a world anew.
I did not dare to blink as the tears fell
For fear it would not be as beautiful when I
opened my eyes.

Save Our Souls

There is no more grief, no more longing.
In that moment, there was only calm.

The happiness of a journey is not in the traveling
itself,
it's in the familiarity of homecoming.

I had taken to the waters to find a new life.
I sailed around this world of mine, only to end
up finding myself.

And once you know yourself, can you ever
really be lost?

Salvation

I am at peace now.
I trust myself in all my pieces.

I learned to let go,
to hold steady,
and to believe.

Days have come and gone,
but I remain.

To love is all I have,
and all I need.